I0966776

The Heart of Autumn

The

Poems for the Season of Reflection

Heart

Selected by Robert Atwan

of

Introduction by Rosanna Warren

Autumn

Beacon Press · Boston

BEACON PRESS
25 Beacon Street
Boston, Massachusetts 02108–2892
www.beacon.org

Beacon Press books are published under the auspices of the Unitarian Universalist Association of Congregations.

Printed in the United States of America

06 05 04 03 02 8 7 6 5 4 3 2 1

This book is printed on acid-free paper that meets the uncoated paper ANSI/NISO specifications for permanence as revised in 1992.

Text design and composition by Christopher Kuntze.

LIBRARY OF CONGRESS CATALOGING-IN-PUBLICATION DATA

The heart of autumn : poems for the season of reflection / selected by Robert Atwan ; introduction by Rosanna Warren.
p. cm.
ISBN 0-8070-6862-4 (Hardcover : alk. paper)
1. Autumn—poetry. 2. American poetry. 3. English poetry. I. Atwan, Robert.
PS595.A89H43 2003
811.008'033—dc21 200301435

CONTENTS

ROSANNA WARREN

Introduction

Two great motifs play the *basso continuo* under the melodies of this anthology: the biblical recognition, in the Book of Job and in Isaiah, that all flesh is grass, and its Homeric corollary in *The Iliad* when Glaukos declares, "As is the generation of leaves, so is that of humanity." The poetry of autumn is inherently elegiac, and inherently vegetal. For all its anxious observation of weather and plant life, it is also philosophical, devoted to parsing and translating the perennial lesson of our deathwardness. Each of the poems collected here registers a form of that knowing, and some explicitly organize themselves around the verb "to know."

Siegfried Sassoon's "Autumn" most clearly acknowledges the biblical and Homeric thesis, hearing in the October wind "a voice that grieves" for the massacred soldiers of the First World War: "Their lives are like the leaves / Scattered in flocks of ruin. . . ." Archibald MacLeish more subtly embodies that mortal knowledge in his "Immortal Autumn," punning on "Now," "No," and "Know," the sly syllables making their own argument phonetically: "Now / No more . . ."; "We are alone: there are no evening birds: we know. . . ." MacLeish has rung his changes on the ancient tradition he seems to have heard in "a dead man's cry from autumn long since gone," turning lament into a jubilate: "I praise the flower-barren fields," "I praise the fall."

The effort of coming to know, through time, provides the skeletal structure of W. S. Merwin's "Under the Day." An x-ray of the poem would read, "To come back like autumn . . . is to waken backward . . . and recognize." His poem brings us to a recognition that cannot be named, and that yields to a new way of seeing, an innocent presentness. Edna St. Vincent Millay, for her part, dramatizes her knowledge in "Autumn Daybreak" ("I know—for I can hear the hiss") as a form of penury, "made known / More by the meagre light increased." This question of knowing brings me to my father's poem: Robert Penn Warren's "Heart of Autumn" presses hard on the verb in both question and statement, playing the human quest for knowledge against the instinctual knowledge of the wild geese: "I have known time and distance, but not why I am here." Frost, in "My November Guest," teasingly splits his knowledge not between man and bird, but between his feminine Sorrow and the poem's male speaker, suggesting "Not yesterday I learned to know"; whereas Jorie Graham's "Mind" takes the challenge head on, seeing the actions of rain and leaves as figures for acts of cognition with their own intimations of mortality as the mind imagines itself entering the ground, "more easily in pieces, / and all the richer for it." The book concludes in a crescendo of knowing with Richard Wilbur and Gerard Manley Hopkins. In the contradictory intuitions of mind and body in Wilbur's wittily titled "In the Elegy Season," the mind leans back toward summer while the body senses already the vigorous advent of spring. Hopkins's great poem "Spring and Fall," which justly closes this book, filters adult knowledge through the child's grief, supplying in the plenitude of invented language—wanwood, leafmeal—some compensation for the subtractions the child fears.

Knowledge, in most of the poems collected here, yields to a drama of utterance. The tone ranges greatly. Some autumnal poets are stirred, in contemplating the sublimity of transience, to a correspondent sublimity of voice. Shelley strikes the highest note in "Ode to the West Wind," famously demanding of the wind, "Make me thy lyre," and dreaming for his own voice "the trumpet of a prophecy." MacLeish, in "Immortal Knowledge," works himself up from the "grave and level voice" of his first line to a cry by the end. But other poets wrest a masterful quietness from nature's withdrawals. Wordsworth finds, in his sonnet "September 1815," "a season potent to renew, / 'Mid frost and snow, the instinctive joys of song." Even more quietly, e.e. cummings reflects the fall's reductiveness in his brilliantly pared down visual poem "[l(a]" with its lines of one or two letters, in which the leaf falls in a parenthesis within the word "loneliness," and smaller words are discovered, dislocated, within larger ones. William Virgil Davis honors the season by reducing his sonnet to thirteen unrhymed lines and stripping lyric song down to laconic saying: "Someday, I may get around / to saying what I've been thinking for months."

Autumn brings into focus the paradox at the heart of being: our knowledge that we are going, our illusion that we will stay. Art is one way we humans have been trying to stay, for millennia, as Shakespeare recorded so well in his autumnal poem, Sonnet 73 ("That time of year thou mayst in me behold / When yellow leaves, or none, or few, do hang / Upon those boughs which shake against the cold . . ."). This poem is not collected here, nor need it be; it has been so deeply absorbed into the English sense of autumn in our bones. Its last line, "To love that well which thou must leave ere long," focuses the essential contradiction. A.R. Ammons's "Equinox" beautifully acts out this paradox; it figures our going and our staying in the play between free verse and the final resonant pentameter, which lodges the poem's modernity within a much older tradition: "and what we hoped would stay we yield to change." Ammons draws his power from the balance struck between "stay" and "change," between "hoped" and "yield." Like Yeats's wild swans, the season is both eternal and migratory. To live fully in autumn is to live in that equilibrium. It is also to feel poignantly the collaboration of fullness and emptiness, as Keats does in "To Autumn." Except for certain odes of Horace, there may be no greater psalm to passage and change than this poem in which time and language take on the material consistency of crushed apple pulp, becoming a kind of thick and intoxicating ooze in the unconventional plurals: "Thou watchest the last oozings hours by hours."

If poems matter, it must be because they return us, however briefly, to fully integrated states of awareness. And of what should we be more aware than of our mysterious transience, in harmony with the natural transience to which we belong? This book has the generosity to give that passing a provisional shape. It is as if we could hold sunlight in our hands. And make a melody of it.

The Heart of Autumn

Season Due

They are unforgiving and do not ask mercy, these last
of the season's flowers: chrysanthemums, brash
marigolds, fat sultan dahlias a-nod

in rain. It is
September. Pansy
freaked with jet be

damned: it takes this radiant bitterness to
stand, to take the throb of sky, now sky
is cold, falls bodily, assaults. In tangled

conclave, spiky-
leaved, they
wait. The news

is fatal. Leaf by leaf, petal
by petal, they brazen out this chill
which has felled already gentler flowers and herbs

and now probes
these veins for a last
mortal volley of

cadmium orange, magenta, a last acrid flood
of perfume that will drift in the air here once more,
yet once more, when these stubborn flowers have died.

A. R. AMMONS

Equinox

I went out to cut a last batch of zinnias this
morning from the back fencerow and got my shanks
chilled for sure: furrowy dark gray clouds with
separating fringes of blue sky-grass: and dew

beaded up heavier than the left-overs of rain:
in the zinnias, in each of two, a bumblebee
stirring in slow-motion. Trying to unwind
the webbed drug of cold, buzzing occasionally but

with a dry rattle: bees die with the burnt honey
at their mouths, at least: the fact's established:
it is not summer now and the simmering buzz is out of
heat: the zucchini blossoms falling show squash

overgreen with stunted growth: the snapdragons have
suckered down into a blossom or so: we passed
into dark last week the even mark of day and night
and what we hoped would stay we yield to change.

Equinox

Clouds go over. The maples flare again.
In the garden the last bright asters
blaze in the autumn air
the way my skin burned
when you turned to me
in the chill breeze off the lake.

The days are cool now,
the nights are deep, and long.
At the feeder a red-winged blackbird
has come in from the fields
and sorts among the seeds.
A rare visitor—
even if he finds what he wants,
he'll never stay here.

These are the last days.
Already the stalks of lilies
have withered, and the gold petals
of the rose melt on the grass.
But the sky flames, more intense.
I didn't see it coming.
For the few days you were here with me,
all the familiar warnings disappeared.

PENELOPE SHUTTLE

September

The leaf-watcher's month,
if she can bear to

The year changing its mind,
voluble as an older bride

The year undergoing pears

September being also a floating classroom
for studying the great lakes

September,
who gives anyone who asks

a guided tour of the year,
the month who keeps all year's promises,

leaf by leaf

ARCHIBALD MACLEISH

Immortal Autumn

I speak this poem now with grave and level voice
In praise of autumn, of the far-horn-winding fall.

I praise the flower-barren fields, the clouds, the tall
Unanswering branches where the wind makes sullen noise.

I praise the fall: it is the human season.
Now
No more the foreign sun does meddle at our earth,
Enforce the green and bring the fallow land to birth,
Nor winter yet weigh all with silence the pine bough,

But now in autumn with the black and outcast crows
Share we the spacious world: the whispering year is gone:
There is more room to live now: the once secret dawn
Comes late by daylight and the dark unguarded goes.

Between the mutinous brave burning of the leaves
And winter's covering of our hearts with his deep snow
We are alone: there are no evening birds: we know
The naked moon: the tame stars circle at our eaves.

It is the human season. On this sterile air
Do words outcarry breath: the sound goes on and on.
I hear a dead man's cry from autumn long since gone.

I cry to you beyond upon this bitter air.

Summer begins to have the look

Summer begins to have the look
Peruser of enchanting Book
Reluctantly but sure perceives
A gain upon the backward leaves—

Autumn begins to be inferred
By millinery of the cloud
Or deeper color in the shawl
That wraps the everlasting hill.

The eye begins its avarice
A meditation chastens speech
Some Dyer of a distant tree
Resumes his gaudy industry.

Conclusion is the course of All
At *most* to be perennial
And then elude stability
Recalls to immortality.

MARY JO SALTER

On Removing Summer from the Public Gardens

—Geraniums, weren't they? And
was it yesterday that x'd
their exhuming? Another
summer gone, and autumn brings

its reproachful litany:
you'll never learn botany,
you'll never learn Latin. What's
happened to the gardener

who held summer in such high
esteem? Working bare-chested
even in rain, but driven
by the calendar like hay-

fever or horseflies, he must
have bundled up his tools, and
headed south with the birds. Now
a squirrel quivers a tail

of smoke, serving himself one
acorn in its own brown bowl;
from the pond, where ducks and Swan
Boats paddled in currents of

their own making, gapes a silence
not of frozen water, but
no water at all. The drained
tub, whose gradient is such

leaves beach on its rim like fish,
is deep enough to suggest
a moat between you and things
you see coming; the trumped-up

island of earth, rock and tree
could be a lion's turf—zoo
for the predator, raw-eyed
Winter, pacing and staring.

Hare Drummer

Do the boys and girls still go to Siever's
For cider, after school, in late September?
Or gather hazel nuts among the thickets
On Aaron Hatfield's farm when the frosts begin?
For many times with the laughing girls and boys
Played I along the road and over the hills
When the sun was low and the air was cool,
Stopping to club the walnut tree
Standing leafless against a flaming west.
Now, the smell of the autumn smoke,
And the dropping acorns,
And the echoes about the vales
Bring dreams of life. They hover over me.
They question me:
Where are those laughing comrades?
How many are with me, how many
In the old orchards along the way to Siever's,
And in the woods that overlook
The quiet water?

September Pitch

Enter autumn as you would
a closing door. Quickly,
cautiously. Look for something inside
that promises color, but be wary
of its cast—a desolate reflection,
an indelible tint.
What is it?
Thieves who steal thoughts
cannot answer. They roam the distracted space
between madness and resolve,
madness and calm.
Let me take you out of this room.
Let me take you to a different season,
one distillate, and beige.
There is too much motion here, too much
color, and voices not yours.
Mama, the autumn is deep.
Its pitch is only beginning, and will brighten
before the end. Brighten
into darkness,
or into spring.

ALAN MICHAEL PARKER

The Geese

October. The sky is cool
and ripe. All day the light
thins to a filigree:
skein of geese, leaf,
cold stream. This is
a fine time, the year
in a jeweler's glass.

Two ideas: I will be
more like the world,
or less. More would mean
smaller measures of success,
each moment as a ripple
on the sharp surface of a pond:
a brown trout nods
and preens, gnats swarm
in a last daze, a frog
flabbergasts himself.
There I am in each;
vain, docile, and afraid—
but ready to forget the single
act, as I act.

Less like the world,
the man rakes his leaves,
a sum of himself.
Up above, a sycamore
scrawls its scrimshaw
in the wind, erased by wind;
balloons from the high
school football game
soar to a speck. Less
like the world, I am
captain of this glass
body, sailing. And if
I break before I wake. . .

Don't forget the geese,
the cloud commands the house.
And the house shudders
in its gutters and drains.
I am less like the geese,
more or less like the world;
a ripple on a pond,
captain of the day.

Simple Autumnal

The measured blood beats out the year's delay.
The tearless eyes and heart, forbidden grief,
Watch the burned, restless, but abiding leaf,
The brighter branches arming the bright day.

The cone, the curving fruit should fall away,
The vine stem crumble, ripe grain know its sheaf.
Bonded to time, fires should have done, be brief,
But, serfs to sleep, they glitter and they stay.

Because not last nor first, grief in its prime
Wakes in the day, and hears of life's intent.
Sorrow would break the seal stamped over time
And set the baskets where the bough is bent.

Full season's come, yet filled trees keep the sky
And never scent the ground where they must lie.

Autumn

October's bellowing anger breaks and cleaves
The bronzed battalions of the stricken wood
In whose lament I hear a voice that grieves
For battle's fruitless harvest, and the feud
Of outraged men. Their lives are like the leaves
Scattered in flocks of ruin, tossed and blown
Along the westering furnace flaring red.
O martyred youth and manhood overthrown,
The burden of your wrongs is on my head.

Under the Day

To come back like autumn
to the moss on the stones
after many seasons
to recur as a face
backlit on the surface
of a dark pool one day
after the year has turned
from the summer it saw
while the first yellow leaves
stare from their forgetting
and the branches grow spare

is to waken backward
down through the still water
knowing without touching
all that was ever there
and has been forgotten
and recognize without
name or understanding

without believing or
holding or direction
in the way that we see
at each moment the air

Autumn Daybreak

Cold wind of autumn, blowing loud
At dawn, a fortnight overdue,
Jostling the doors, and tearing through
My bedroom to rejoin the cloud,

I know—for I can hear the hiss
And scrape of leaves along the floor—
How many boughs, lashed bare by this,
Will rake the cluttered sky once more.

Tardy, and somewhat south of east,
The sun will rise at length, made known
More by the meagre light increased
Than by a disk in a splendour shown;

When, having but to turn my head,
Through the stripped maple I shall see,
Bleak and remembered, patched with red,
The hill all summer hid from me.

WILLIAM WORDSWORTH

September, 1815

While not a leaf seems faded; while the fields,
With ripening harvest prodigally fair,
In brightest sunshine bask; this nipping air,
Sent from some distant clime where Winter wields
His icy scimitar, a foretaste yields
Of bitter change, and bids the flowers beware;
And whispers to the silent birds, “Prepare
Against the threatening foe your trustiest shields.”
For me, who under kindlier laws belong
To Nature’s tuneful quire, this rustling dry
Through leaves yet green, and yon crystalline sky,
Announce a season potent to renew,
’Mid frost and snow, the instinctive joys of song,
And nobler cares than listless summer knew.

Auto-Autumn

What happened to sweet heat, the sneezeweed,
the luna moth and gingham sleeve, sipped Slurpies
and reedy kayaks, the sponge-bathed trees? Why
are the nights so flustered and furrowed,

dusks crimped by crooked V's of snow geese
bored with palmettos? Why does the full moon
pinprick the draft, neurotic winds reentering therapy,
the light, an ash blonde with a melanoma scare,

suddenly draped? And why can't one escape
this surly schedule, or, like a mule chained to a wheat
thrasher, adjust to the cycle? But, oh no, optimism

is unavailable, gone crop-dusting below Mexico,
leaving the crotchety with self-help manuals on how
to let go, stay thin, be alone, and feel wonderful.

Heart of Autumn

Wind finds the northwest gap, fall comes.
Today, under gray cloud-scud over gray
Wind-flicker of forest, in perfect formation, wild geese
Head for a land of warm water, the *boom*, the lead pellet.

Some crumple in air, fall. Some stagger, recover control,
Then take the last glide for a far glint of water. None
Knows what has happened. Now, today, watching
How tirelessly *V* upon *V* arrows the season's logic,

Do I know my own story? At least, they know
When the hour comes for the great wing-beat. Sky-strider,
Star-strider—they rise, and the imperial utterance,
Which cries out for distance, quivers in the wheeling sky.

That much they know, and their nature know
The path of pathlessness, with all the joy
Of destiny fulfilling its own name.
I have known time and distance, but not why I am here.

Path of logic, path of folly, all
The same—and I stand, my face lifted now skyward,
Hearing the high beat, my arms outstretched in the tingling
Process of transformation, and soon tough legs,

With folded feet, trail in the sounding vacuum of passage,
And my heart is impacted with a fierce impulse
To unwordable utterance—
Toward sunset, at a great height.

The Fall of Leaves

The green has suddenly
Divided to pure flame,
Leaf-tongued from tree to tree.
Yea, where we stood it came.

This change may have no name,
Yet it was like a word
Spoken, and none to blame,
Alive where shadow stirred.

So was the instant blurred.
But as we waited there
The slow cry of a bird
Built up a scheme of air.

The vision of despair
Starts at the moment's bound,
Seethes from the vibrant air
With slow autumnal sound

Into the burning ground.

E. E. CUMMINGS

l(a

le
af
fa

ll

s)
one
l

iness

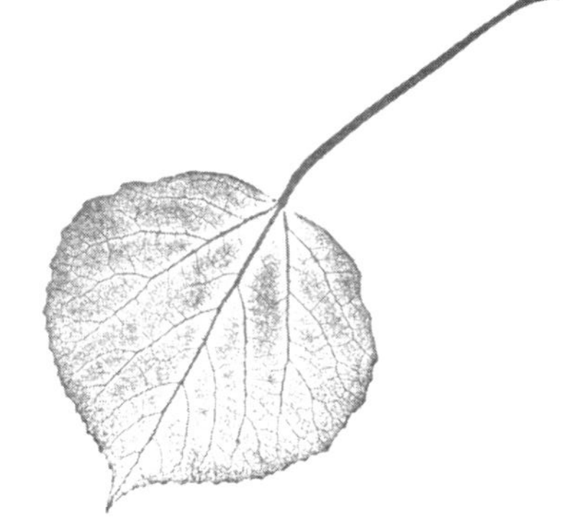

Proud Riders

We rode hard, and brought the cattle from brushy springs,
From heavy dying thickets, leaves wet as snow;
From high places, white-grassed and dry in the wind;
Draws where the quaken-asps were yellow and white,
And the leaves spun and spun like money spinning.
We poured them on to the trail, and rode for town.

Men in the fields leaned forward in the wind,
Stood in the stubble and watched the cattle passing.
The wind bowed all, the stubble shook like a shirt.
We threw the reins by the yellow and black fields, and rode,
And came, riding together, into the town
Which is by the gray bridge, where the alders are.
The white-barked alder trees dropping big leaves
Yellow and black, into the cold black water.
Children, little cold boys, watched after us—
The freezing wind flapped their clothes like windmill paddles.
Down the flat frosty road we crowded the herd:
High stepped the horses for us, proud riders in autumn.

JOHN KEATS

To Autumn

I

Season of mists and mellow fruitfulness,
Close bosom-friend of the maturing sun;
Conspiring with him how to load and bless
With fruit the vines that round the thatch-eves run;
To bend with apples the mossed cottage-trees,
And fill all fruit with ripeness to the core;
To swell the gourd, and plump the hazel shells
With a sweet kernel; to set budding more,
And still more, later flowers for the bees,
Until they think warm days will never cease,
For Summer has o'er-brimmed their clammy cells.

II

Who hath not seen thee oft amid thy store?
Sometimes whoever seeks abroad may find
Thee sitting careless on a granary floor,
Thy hair soft-lifted by the winnowing wind;
Or on a half-reaped furrow sound asleep,
Drowsed with the fume of poppies, while thy hook
Spares the next swath and all its twinèd flowers:
And sometimes like a gleaner thou dost keep
Steady thy laden head across a brook;
Or by a cider-press, with patient look,
Thou watchest the last oozings hours by hours.

III

Where are the songs of Spring? Aye, where are they?
  Think not of them, thou hast thy music too,—
While barred clouds bloom the soft-dying day,
  And touch the stubble-plains with rosy hue;
Then in a wailful choir the small gnats mourn
  Among the river sallows, borne aloft
    Or sinking as the light wind lives or dies;
And full-grown lambs loud bleat from hilly bourn;
  Hedge-crickets sing; and now with treble soft
  The red-breast whistles from a garden-croft;
    And gathering swallows twitter in the skies.

CARL SANDBURG

Falltime

Gold of a ripe oat straw, gold of a southwest moon,
Canada-thistle blue and flimmering larkspur blue,
Tomatoes shining in the October sun with red hearts,
Shining five and six in a row on a wooden fence,
Why do you keep wishes on your faces all day long,
Wishes like women with half-forgotten lovers going to new cities?
What is there for you in the birds, the birds, the birds, crying down
 on the north wind in September—acres of birds spotting the
 air going south?

Is there something finished? And some new beginning on the way?

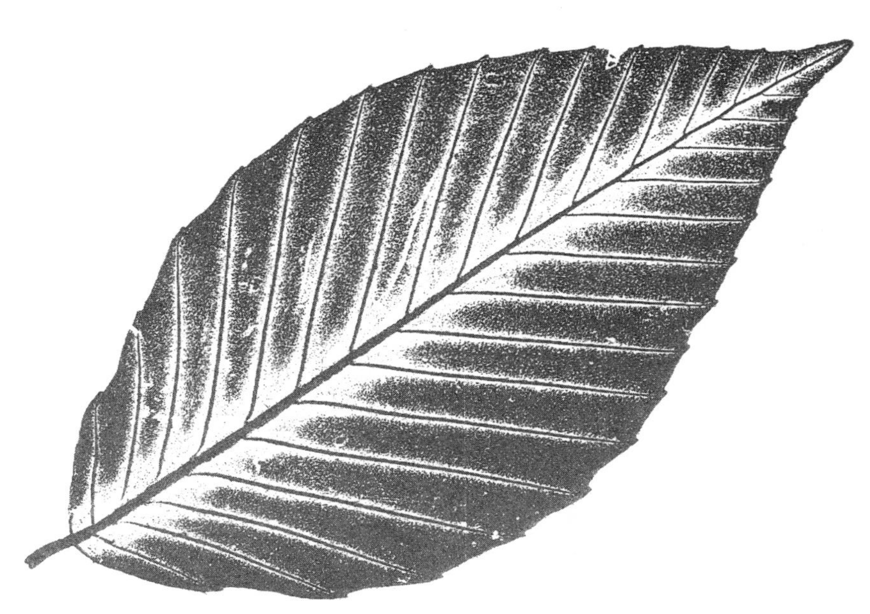

CARL SANDBURG

Autumn Movement

I cried over beautiful things, knowing no beautiful thing lasts.

The field of cornflower yellow is a scarf at the neck of the copper
sunburned woman, the mother of the year, the taker of seeds.

The northwest wind comes and the yellow is torn full of holes, new
beautiful things come in the first spit of snow on the northwest
wind, and the old things go, not one lasts.

The First Autumn

For E.M.S.

Though in a little while
You will be dead again
After this first rehearsal
Since then and all the pain,
Still it's not death that spends
So tenderly this treasure
In leaf-rich golden winds,
But life in lavish measure.

October spends the aster,
Riches of purple, blue,
Lavender, white, that glow
In ragged starry cluster.
Then, when November comes,
Shaggy chrysanthemums,
Salmon-pink, saffron yellow,
All coppers bright and mellow,
Stand up against the frost
And never count the cost.

No, it’s not death this year
Since then and all the pain.
It’s life we harvest here
(Sun on the crimson vine).
The garden speaks your name.
We drink your joys like wine.

The Wild Swans at Coole

The trees are in their autumn beauty,
The woodland paths are dry,
Under the October twilight the water
Mirrors a still sky;
Upon the brimming water among the stones
Are nine-and-fifty swans.

The nineteenth autumn has come upon me
Since I first made my count;
I saw, before I had well finished,
All suddenly mount
And scatter wheeling in great broken rings
Upon their clamorous wings.

I have looked upon those brilliant creatures,
And now my heart is sore.
All's changed since I, hearing at twilight,
The first time on this shore,
The bell-beat of their wings above my head,
Trod with a lighter tread.

Unwearied still, lover by lover,
They paddle in the cold
Companionable streams or climb the air;
Their hearts have not grown old;

Passion or conquest, wander where they will,
Attend upon them still.

But now they drift on the still water,
Mysterious, beautiful;
Among what rushes will they build,
By what lake's edge or pool
Delight men's eyes when I awake some day
To find they have flown away?

MARIANNE BORUCH

Leaves in Fall

They come down, straight down or crooked,
fast or drunken. Wind might do it,
might call the cruel trick but they're
starving anyway, light's sugar
nothing so sweet now,
and then this mysterious business
of turning a drastic color. I rake.
I rake the damn sad things
all morning, past lunch.
What was I thinking?

        That certain things
have to be done. That the earth
orbits slowly. That beauty gives up
its beauty. Huge piles of it—
maple's yellow, the elm's ghost gray,
hackberry with its sulfurous boils
curled tight. Maybe someone else
said this: the sky is a pearl, darkening.
Or this: it's bad milk, not a cloud
against anything.

        So I rake
and drag it all on a tarp to the curb, the heavy
scrape scrape of it past birdbath

and trellis, past the cockeyed seasick mums,
past the torn shade of playroom, study, frontroom
where the old piano sits
completely out of tune. Dark inkling
it was, to the nether world
of the minor key.
                                        The dead
lean forward.

Ode to the West Wind

O wild West Wind, thou breath of Autumn's being,
  Thou, from whose unseen presence the leaves dead
Are driven, like ghosts from an enchanter fleeing,
  Yellow, and black, and pale, and hectic red,
Pestilence-stricken multitudes! O thou
  Who chariotest to their dark wintry bed
The winged seeds, where they lie cold and low,
  Each like a corpse within its grave, until
Thine azure sister of the Spring shall blow
  Her clarion o'er the dreaming earth, and fill
(Driving sweet buds like flocks to feed in air)
  With living hues and odors plain and hill:
Wild Spirit, which art moving everywhere;
Destroyer and preserver; hear, oh hear!

Thou on whose stream, mid the steep sky's commotion,
  Loose clouds like earth's decaying leaves are shed,
Shook from the tangled boughs of heaven and ocean,
  Angels of rain and lightning! there are spread
On the blue surface of thine airy surge,
  Like the bright hair uplifted from the head
Of some fierce Maenad, ev'n from the dim verge
  Of the horizon to the zenith's height,
The locks of the approaching storm. Thou dirge
  Of the dying year, to which this closing night

Will be the dome of a vast sepulchre,
  Vaulted with all thy congregated might
Of vapors, from whose solid atmosphere
Black rain, and fire, and hail, will burst: oh hear!

Thou, who didst waken from his summer-dreams
  The blue Mediterranean, where he lay,
Lull'd by the coil of his crystalline streams,
  Beside a pumice isle in Baiae's bay,
And saw in sleep old palaces and towers
  Quivering within the wave's intenser day.
All overgrown with azure moss, and flowers
  So sweet, the sense faints picturing them! Thou
For whose path the Atlantic's level powers
  Cleave themselves into chasms, while far below
The sea-blooms and the oozy woods which wear
  The sapless foliage of the ocean, know
Thy voice, and suddenly grow gray with fear
And tremble and despoil themselves: oh hear!

If I were a dead leaf thou mightest bear;
  If I were a swift cloud to fly with thee;
A wave to pant beneath thy power, and share
  The impulse of thy strength, only less free
Than Thou, O uncontrollable! If even
  I were as in my boyhood, and could be

The comrade of thy wanderings over heaven,
  As then, when to outstrip thy skyey speed
Scarce seem'd a vision,—I would ne'er have striven
  As thus with thee in prayer in my sore need.
Oh! lift me as a wave, a leaf, a cloud!
  I fall upon the thorns of life! I bleed!
A heavy weight of hours has chain'd and bow'd
One too like thee—tameless, and swift, and proud.

Make me thy lyre, ev'n as the forest is:
  What if my leaves are falling like its own!
The tumult of thy mighty harmonies
  Will take from both a deep autumnal tone,
Sweet though in sadness. Be thou, Spirit fierce,
  My spirit! be thou me, impetuous one!
Drive my dead thoughts over the universe,
  Like wither'd leaves, to quicken a new birth;
And, by the incantation of this verse,
  Scatter, as from an unextinguish'd hearth
Ashes and sparks, my words among mankind!
  Be through my lips to unawaken'd earth
The trumpet of a prophecy! O Wind,
If Winter comes, can Spring be far behind?

ADELAIDE CRAPSEY

November Night

Listen.
With faint dry sound,
Like steps of passing ghosts,
The leaves, frost-crisp'd, break from the trees
And fall.

My November Guest

My Sorrow, when she's here with me,
  Thinks these dark days of autumn rain
Are beautiful as days can be;
She loves the bare, the withered tree;
  She walks the sodden pasture lane.

Her pleasure will not let me stay.
  She talks and I am fain to list:
She's glad the birds are gone away,
She's glad her simple worsted gray
  Is silver now with clinging mist.

The desolate, deserted trees,
  The faded earth, the heavy sky,
The beauties she so truly sees,
She thinks I have no eye for these,
  And vexes me for reason why.

Not yesterday I learned to know
  The love of bare November days
Before the coming of the snow,
But it were vain to tell her so,
  And they are better for her praise.

Turn Me to My Yellow Leaves

Turn me to my yellow leaves,
I am better satisfied;
There is nothing in me grieves—
That was never born—and died.
Let me be a scarlet flame
On a windy autumn morn,
I, who never had a name,
Nor from a breathing image born.
From the margin let me fall
Where the farthest stars sink down.
And the void consume me,—all
Into nothingness to drown.
Let me dream my dream entire,
Withered as an autumn leaf—
Let me have my vain desire,
Vain—as it is brief!

Firewalking Through November

If sunlight touched
the ground earlier, I wasn't there
to see. The fallen leaves are stuck
in their sullen swirl
like thoughts of a mind
that can't stop mulling over the lack

of possibilities. In the past half-hour,
they've gathered,
leaning against a gritty wall
like street-corner vagrants.
They shift in the wind to rasp
a faint protest: nowhere to go

but down. Yet the few gold leaves
that still hang on the trees
are now back-lit
to a transparency
you could passs through
    not just unharmed but warmed.

Think of the word *beneficent*—
like a glance
that happens to catch

the sun's last rays striking a pane,
you hold the afterimage
until you feel you could leap

through fire, that window,
see your way clear
through anything, even a dead season.

WILLIAM VIRGIL DAVIS

Leaves

The leaves have almost completely covered
the backyard, and there are leaves to fall.
The wind whistles through its thin teeth
and no one seems to mind. For weeks we
have watched from windows, seen colors
changing, but not talked about it. One night,
when we went to gather another load
of wood, we heard the dead leaves crunch
beneath our feet. Now a light snow has begun
to touch the trees and the woodpile, first
fingerprinting them, then blurring, blending
everything in. Someday, I may get around
to saying what I've been thinking for months.

Hoar-Frost

In the cloud-gray mornings
I heard the herons flying;
And when I came into my garden,
My silken outer-garment
Trailed over withered leaves.
A dried leaf crumbles at a touch,
But I have seen many Autumns
With herons blowing like smoke
Across the sky.

Mind

The slow overture of rain,
each drop breaking
without breaking into
the next, describes
the unrelenting, syncopated
mind. Not unlike
the hummingbirds
imagining their wings
to be their heart, and swallows
believing the horizon
to be a line they lift
and drop. What is it
they cast for? The poplars,
advancing or retreating,
lose their stature
equally, and yet stand firm,
making arrangements
in order to become
imaginary. The city
draws the mind in streets,
and streets compel it
from their intersections
where a little
belongs to no one. It is
what is driven through

all stationary portions
of the world, gravity's
stake in things. The leaves,
pressed against the dank
window of November
soil, remain unwelcome
till transformed, parts
of a puzzle unsolvable
till the edges give a bit
and soften. See how
then the picture becomes clear,
the mind entering the ground
more easily in pieces,
and all the richer for it.

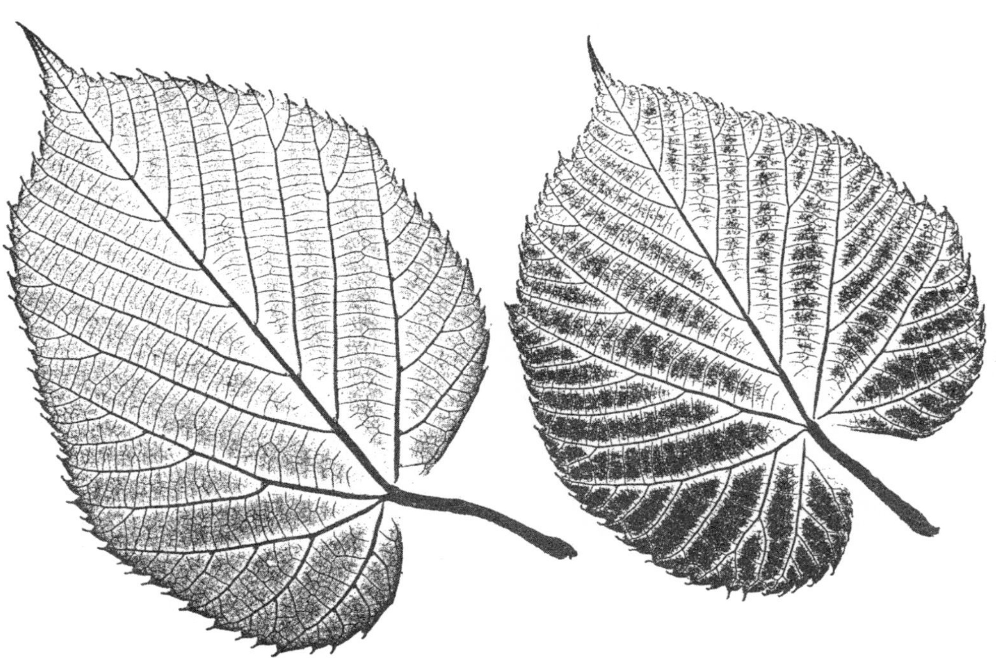

Solitude Late at Night in the Woods

I

The body is like a November birch facing the full moon
And reaching into the cold heavens.
In these trees there is no ambition, no sodden body,
    no leaves,
Nothing but bare trunks climbing like cold fire!

II

My last walk in the trees has come. At dawn
I must return to the trapped fields,
To the obedient earth.
The trees shall be reaching all the winter.

III

It is a joy to walk in the bare woods.
The moonlight is not broken by the heavy leaves.
The leaves are down, and touching the soaked earth,
Giving off the odor that partridges love.

November Fifth, Riverside Drive

The sky a shock, the ginkgoes yellow fever,
I wear the day out walking. November, and still
light stuns the big bay windows on West End
Avenue, the park brims over with light like a bowl
and on the river
a sailboat quivers like a white leaf in the wind.

How like an eighteenth-century painting, this
year's decorous decline: the sun
still warms the aging marble porticos
and scrolled pavilions past which an old man,
black-coated apparition of Voltaire,
flaps on his constitutional. "Clear air,
clear mind"—as if he could outpace
darkness scything home like a flock of crows.

RICHARD WILBUR

In the Elegy Season

Haze, char, and the weather of All Souls':
A giant absence mopes upon the trees:
Leaves cast in casual potpourris
Whisper their scents from pits and cellar-holes.

Or brewed in gulleys, steeped in wells, they spend
In chilly steam their last aromas, yield
From shallow hells a revenance of field
And orchard air. And now the envious mind

Which could not hold the summer in my head
While bounded by that blazing circumstance
Parades these barrens in a golden trance,
Remembering the wealthy season dead,

And by an autumn inspiration makes
A summer all its own. Green boughs arise
Through all the boundless backward of the eyes,
And the soul bathes in warm conceptual lakes.

Less proud than this, my body leans an ear
Past cold and colder weather after wings'
Soft commotion, the sudden race of springs,
The goddess' tread heard on the dayward stair,

Longs for the brush of the freighted air, for smells
Of grass and cordial lilac, for the sight
Of green leaves building into the light
And azure water hoisting out of wells.

Spring and Fall: To a Young Child

Márgarét, are you gríeving
Over Goldengrove unleaving?
Leáves, líke the things of man, you
With your fresh thoughts care for, can you?
Áh! ás the heart grows older
It will come to such sights colder
By and by, nor spare a sigh
Though worlds of wanwood leafmeal lie;
And yet you will weep and know why.
Now no matter, child, the name:
Sórrow's spríngs áre the same.
Nor mouth had, no nor mind, expressed
What heart heard of, ghost guessed:
It ís the blight man was born for,
It is Margaret you mourn for.

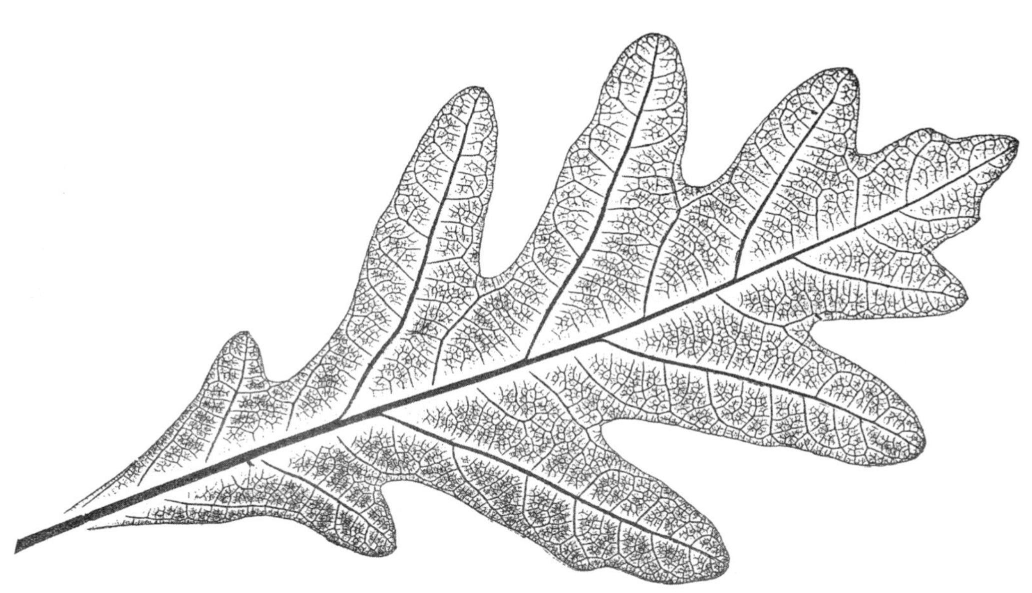

BIOGRAPHICAL NOTES BY ROBERT ATWAN

Although he wrote poems on just about every topic under the sun, **A. R. Ammons** (1926–2001) was especially sensitive to the outdoor world—the seasons, the weather, the woods, the endless varieties of sky above. His keen love of nature is reflected in many of the titles he gave his collections: *Expressions of Sea Level* (1964), *Uplands* (1970), *The Snow Poems* (1977), *A Coast of Trees* (1981), and *Lake-Effect Country* (1983). Raised on a North Carolina farm, Ammons graduated Wake Forest University with a degree in science. The recipient of numerous awards, including two National Book Awards and a MacArthur Fellowship, Ammons taught at Cornell University from 1964 until his retirement in 1998.

A former staff photographer for United Press International, **Star Black** was born in Coronado, California, grew up in Washington D.C., and Hawaii, and received her education at both Wellesley and Brooklyn Colleges. Her poems have appeared in many journals, and her books of poetry include *Double Time* (1995), *Waterworn* (1995), *October for Idas*, (1997), and *Balefire* (1999). A professional photographer in New York City and Sag Harbor, Long Island, she also co-founded a popular Manhattan poetry reading series with David Lehman, with whom she has published a collection from the readings, *The KGB Bar Book of Poems* (2000).

The poet, essayist, and translator **Robert Bly** was born on a farm in Madison, Minnesota, in 1926. After servicing in the U.S. Navy, Bly attended St. Olaf's College and Harvard, and he earned an M.A. from the writing program at the University of Iowa. Celebrated for his readings and lectures, Bly has published numerous prizewinning volumes of poetry, including *The Light Around the Body* (1967), a collection of anti–Vietnam War poems that received the National Book Award. He is still perhaps best-known for such early volumes as *Silence in the Snowy Fields* (1962), his first book, which is characterized by the quiet landscapes and meditative rhythms we find in "Solitude Late at Night in the Woods." In the 1980s Bly began exploring what he called the "new male consciousness" and in 1990 published a best-selling book on the subject, *Iron John: A Book about Men*. Recent volumes of poetry include *What Have I Ever Lost by Dying?: Collected Prose Poems* (1992); *Snowbanks North of the House* (1999); and *The Night Abraham Called to the Stars* (2001).

A long-time poetry reviewer for *The New Yorker*, **Louise Bogan** (1897–1970) earned a serious reputation as both a critic and a poet. Born in Maine and educated in Boston schools, she married in 1916 and within a few years had a child, separated, and moved to Greenwich Village. There she formed associations with various literary groups and magazines, and she became one of the first Americans to undergo intensive psychoanalytic treatment, therapy she continued throughout her life. Her collections include *Body of this Death* (1923), *Dark Summer* (1929), *The Sleeping Fury* (1937), and *The Blue Estuaries: Poems 1923–1968* (1968).

Born in Chicago in 1950, **Marianne Boruch** is the author of four collections of poetry: *View from the Gazebo* (1983), *Descendant* (1989), *Moss Burning* (1993), and *A Stick that Breaks and Breaks* (1997). She teaches in the MFA Program at Purdue University. *Poetry's Old Air*, her collection of essays on poets and poetry, was published in 1995.

The poet, editor, and anthologist **William Stanley Braithwaite** (1878–1962) was born in Boston to West Indian parents, raised in an Anglican atmosphere, and educated at the Boston Latin School. He briefly edited *Colored American Magazine* and then became a noted columnist and literary editor of the *Boston Evening Transcript*, where he conducted one of the earliest and most astute interviews with Robert Frost. For many years, Braithwaite edited an influential annual anthology of magazine verse and earned a national reputation as a critic and reviewer. From 1933 to 1945, he taught at Atlanta University, where he began forming a closer association with fellow African-American writers. Braithwaite published three works of fiction, a biographical study of the Brontës, and three volumes of poetry, *Lyrics of Life and Love* (1904), *The House of Falling Leaves* (1908), and *Selected Poems* (1948). *The House Under Arcturus*, his autobiography, appeared in 1941.

The daughter of a well-known minister whose "heretical" views led to his removal from the Episcopal Church, **Adelaide Crapsey** (1878–1914) was raised in Rochester, New York, and, after graduating from Vassar College in 1901, studied archaeology in Rome. Chronic ill health interfered with her academic career and, after a brief time teaching poetry at Smith College and several years of medical treatment, she died of tuberculosis, leaving two books to be published posthumously, *Verse* (1915) and *A Study in English Metrics* (1918). One of her best-known poems, "November Night," displays her interest in innovative metrical verse and perfectly illustrates what she termed a "cinquain," an unrhymed five-line stanza with lines of two, four, six, eight, and two syllables.

The son of a Unitarian minister, **E. E. Cummings** (1894–1962) was born in Cambridge, Massachusetts, and received his B.A. and M.A. at Harvard, where he acquired modernist tastes and where his more conventional father taught English and ethics. Cummings's bohemian sensibilities were further encouraged by several years in Paris, where he lived after enlisting in an ambulance corps during WWI. Suspected of spying, he spent a few months in a French internment camp, an experience he memorably reported in *The Enormous Room* (1922). A talented painter, he moved, a year after the publication of his first collection, *Tulips & Chimneys* (1923), to Greenwich Village in hopes of becoming an artist, but he soon discovered he could also apply his visual gifts and experimental disposition to the shape of the poem on the printed page. *The Complete Poems* appeared in 1972.

H. L. Davis (1896–1960) won both the Harper Prize and the Pulitzer Prize in 1935 for *Honey in the Horn*, a frontier novel set in his home state of Oregon. Davis's other novels of the Northwest include *Harp of a Thousand Strings* (1947), *Beulah Land* (1949), *The Winds of Morning* (1952), and *Distant Music* (1957). *The Kettle of Fire* (1959) is a collection of essays celebrating the region. Davis intimately knew and loved the outdoor life, working in the Pacific Northwest as a surveyor, sheriff, and cattle herder, the last occupation inspiring his best-known poem, "Proud Riders." The poem appeared in the volume *Proud Riders* (1942).

An ordained Presbyterian minister, **William Virgil Davis** was born in Canton, Ohio, in 1940. He earned his B.A., M.A., and Ph.D. from Ohio University and also received an M.Div. from Pittsburgh Theological Seminary. His first volume of poems, *One Way to Reconstruct the Scene* (1980) won the prestigious Yale Younger Poets Prize. His other volumes include *The Dark Hours* (1984) and *Winter Light* (1990). The recipient of a John Atherton Fellowship in Poetry and a Lilly Foundation grant, Davis has also published two critical books, *Understanding Robert Bly* (1988) and *Robert Bly: The Poet and His Critics* (1994).

Emily Dickinson (1830–1886) spent most of her life as a recluse in her parents' home in Amherst, Massachusetts, where her father served as treasurer of Amherst College. Although she wrote nearly two thousand poems, only a few were published in her lifetime. The first complete and textually authentic collection of her poetry did not appear until 1955, a publishing event that surely qualifies her as one of America's leading "modern" poets. Through uncanny paths of perception and with remarkable compression, her poems, like momentary flashes of insight, take us to the edges of human thought. Yet, as enigmatic as these mental journeys may seem, they are

firmly rooted in a particular place: "I see—New Englandly . . . ," she once rhymed.

So closely associated is **Robert Frost** (1874–1963) with New England that few people realize he was actually born in San Francisco. He didn't move east until he was eleven, when his father's death left the family penniless. "My November Guest" appeared in Frost's first poetry collection, *A Boy's Will* (1913) as part of a sequence of poems on youth; in this now priceless first edition, Frost included with the poems a series of enigmatic notes that he dropped in all subsequent editions. The note to "My November Guest" reads: "He is in love with being misunderstood."

Born in New York City in 1950, **Jorie Graham** was raised in Italy, where her mother pursued a career as a painter and sculptor and where Graham formed a lifelong interest in the visual arts. After studying philosophy at the Sorbonne, Graham enrolled in Martin Scorsese's famous cinema program at New York University; she worked in television after graduating in 1972. In 1978, she earned an M.F.A. at the University of Iowa, where she went on to teach for many years. Her highly acclaimed volumes of poetry include *Hybrids of Plants and of Ghosts* (1980), *Erosion* (1983), *The End of Beauty* (1987), *Region of Unlikeness* (1991), *Materialism* (1993), *The Errancy* (1997), *Swarm* (2000), and *Never* (2002). In 1996 she received the Pulitzer Prize for *The Dream of the Unified Field: Selected Poems 1974–1994*. A Chancellor of the Academy of American Poets as well as the winner of a MacArthur Fellowship, a Guggenheim Fellowship, and the Morton Dauwen Zabel Award from the American Academy and Institute of Arts and Letters, Graham is now the Boylston Professor of Rhetoric and Oratory at Harvard University.

The author of, most recently, *In Praise of Motels* (1999), **Pamela Steed Hill** was born in 1958 and grew up in Kentucky. She received an M.A. in English from Marshall University in West Virginia and has been published extensively in numerous journals, such as *The Antioch Review*, *Nimrod*, *Chicago Review*, *Epoch*, *Sulphur River Literary Review*, and *Fine Madness*. A three-time nominee for a Pushcart Prize, she is currently at Ohio State University and serves as an editor of Blair Mountain Press in Ashland, Kentucky.

Patricia Hooper is the author of *Other Lives* (1984), which received the Poetry Society of America's Norma Farber First Book Award, *The Flowering Trees* (1995), and *At the Corner of the Eye* (1998). Her poems have appeared in *Poetry*, *The Atlantic Monthly*, *The American Scholar*, *The Hud-*

son Review, The New Criterion, The American Poetry Review, and other magazines. She has also written two children's books.

When the poet Robert Bridges hesitantly edited and published the small posthumous volume of **Gerard Manley Hopkins**'s *Poems* in 1918, he dramatically altered the course of modern poetry. Perhaps the most innovative Victorian poet, Hopkins (1844–1889) was born at Stratford in Essex and educated at Oxford, where he earned highest honors in classics and a reputation as a brilliant scholar. At Oxford he converted to Catholicism and in 1877 was ordained a Jesuit priest. Hopkins burned his early poetry when he entered religious life, and his subsequent output was particularly small. He died of typhoid fever while a professor of classics at University College in Dublin. The title "Spring and Fall" is a triple pun, referring to the earth's diametrical seasons, to the gravitational motion of its creatures, and to Hopkins's own elaborate metrical system of "sprung rhythm" that remains the dominant characteristic of his poetry.

One of the greatest autumn poems was composed over two days in September 1819 by a twenty-three-year-old poet whose medical training convinced him he didn't have long to live. **John Keats** (1795–1821) was born into a fairly prosperous family, though his father's humble origins would later make Keats the butt of Tory snobbery in the literary reviews. When Keats was eight, his father died in a riding accident and then at the age of fourteen his mother died of tuberculosis. Falling under the care of a guardian with a more practical than poetic bent, Keats was apprenticed to a London surgeon to learn medicine, a trade he abandoned in 1817, when he published his first volume of poetry. Soon after losing his brother to tuberculosis in 1818, Keats experienced one of the most remarkable bursts of creativity in English literary history, writing many of his major poems, including "To Autumn," with its ominous evocation of a grim reaper, in less than a year's time. A few months after his twenty-fifth birthday, Keats died in Rome of the family disease that had haunted him for years.

A relative of the poet James Russell Lowell, **Amy Lowell** (1874–1925) was born in Brookline, Massachusetts, the sister of Abbott Lawrence Lowell, who served as Harvard University's president for nearly twenty-five years. Influenced by the Imagist movement, she began publishing experimental and highly visual poems, beginning with *Sword Blades and Poppy Seed* (1914). She became a leading and controversial advocate of the "New Poetry," which she helped promote through criticism, theatrical lecture tours, and collections. Her spirited but disorganized biographical study of John Keats appeared just before her untimely death. Though she received a posthumous Pulitzer Prize for her last volume of poetry, she remains a neglected literary figure, despite recent attention to feminist as well as gay and lesbian studies.

Born in Glencoe, Illinois, **Archibald MacLeish** (1892–1982) graduated from Yale in 1915 and from Harvard Law School in 1919. He interrupted his legal studies to serve in World War I, seeing action at the Second Battle of the Marne and rising to the rank of captain. In 1923, having already published a volume of poetry, he left the practice of law and moved with his wife and family from Boston to France, where he continued to write. Returning to the States in 1928, he served as an editor of *Fortune* magazine before being appointed as the first curator of the Neiman Foundation at Harvard. From 1939 to 1944 he served as Librarian of Congress and afterwards as assistant secretary of state, taking an active role in the creation of UNESCO. In 1962 he retired as Boylston Professor of Oratory and Rhetoric at Harvard, a position he had held since 1949. During this active public life, MacLeish managed to publish extensively and win three Pulitzer Prizes: for his lyrical epic, *Conquistador* (1932), *Collected Poems* (1952), and his verse drama *J.B.* (1958), a Broadway success that also won a Tony Award.

Edgar Lee Masters (1868–1950) grew up in Illinois, near the Spoon River, which served as the site of his best-known collection of poems, *Spoon River Anthology*, a series of loosely interlocking free-verse monologues from 244 inhabitants (such as Hare Drummer) of a local cemetery, all voices from beyond the grave. In his mid-forties when the book was published, Masters had been successfully practicing law in Chicago, where for a number of years he was a partner of the great trial lawyer Clarence Darrow. Masters had published several poetry volumes previously, but with *Spoon River* he hit on an innovative novelistic structure and combined it with a stark colloquial verse form that helped make the book an instant bestseller and one of the most popular volumes of poetry in American literary history. After leaving his law practice, Masters published prolifically—poetry, fiction, drama, biography and autobiography—but nothing ever came close to the success of *Spoon River Anthology*.

William Merwin's first volume of poetry, *A Mask for Janus,* was selected by W. H. Auden for the Yale Younger Poets Award in 1952, not long after Merwin graduated from Princeton. Since then, Merwin, who was born in New York City in 1927 and grew up in Scranton, Pennsylvania, has published many books of poetry, each one since *The Drunk in the Furnace* (1960) marking both a continuation as well as a discontinuation of what came before. As Merwin says: "What I'm really interested in is not what I've written but what I haven't written, the next poem, if there is one." This process of not knowing or unknowing characterizes Merwin's best poetry, which proceeds in a non-deliberative manner that is at once elegant and enigmatic. Perhaps most surprisingly, Merwin can also adapt this unique style to poems with a distinct political purpose. The winner of many awards for his poetry and translations, including the Pulitzer Prize for *The Carrier of Ladders* (1970), Merwin, who now lives in Hawaii, has served as Chancellor of the Academy of American Poets and is the author most recently of *A River Sound* (1999) and a translation of Dante's *Purgatorio* (2000).

One of the most talked-about poets of the 1920s and 30s, **Edna St. Vincent Millay** (1892–1950) was born in Rockland, Maine, and educated at Vassar College, where she graduated in 1917, the same year her first volume of poetry *Renascence* appeared to great acclaim. She moved to Greenwich Village, the stage for much of her highly publicized Bohemian life as well as her work. The first volumes came rapidly: *A Few Figs from Thistles* (1920), *Second April* (1921), and the Pulitzer Prize–winning *The Ballad of the Harp Weaver* (1922). She published many more collections but her reputation rests primarily on these early books, with their dominant fin de siecle theme of someone burning the candle at both ends. Her *Collected Poems* appeared posthumously in 1956.

Alan Michael Parker is the author of three volumes of poetry, *Days Like Prose*, listed by the National Book Critics Circle as a Notable Book of 1997, *The Vandals* (1999), and *Love Song with Motor Vehicles* (2003). He is also a coeditor of *The Routledge Anthology of Cross-Gendered Verse* (1996) and an editor of *Who's Who in Twentieth-Century World Poetry*. Parker was born in 1961, he earned a B.A. at Washington University and an M.F.A. at Columbia University's School of the Arts; he also reviews regularly for *The New Yorker* and writes a monthly column for *The Charlotte Observer*. He received a Pushcart Prize in 1998 and has been awarded fellowships from the New Jersey and Pennsylvania Councils on the Arts. He taught English and creative writing at Rutgers University and Penn State Erie, The Behrend College, before joining the faculty of Davidson College.

Katha Pollitt was born in New York City in 1949 and is in many ways a unique literary figure, having earned a major reputation as both an award-winning lyric poet and a highly influential political essayist. Few American writers have achieved a command of both aesthetics and polemics, and fewer still have managed to keep these endeavors distinct: "What I want in a poem—" Pollitt writes, "one that I read or one that I write—is not an

argument, it's not a statement, it has to do with language." Educated at Harvard and at Columbia School of the Arts, she has been a columnist for *The Nation* since 1994. She won a National Book Critics Circle Award for her 1982 collection of poetry, *Antarctic Traveller*, and has also published several collections of essays, including *Reasonable Creatures* (1994) and *Subject to Debate* (2001). Besides winning a National Magazine Award, she has also received fellowships from the Guggenheim Foundation, the Whiting Foundation, and the National Endowment for the Arts.

Educated at Harvard and Cambridge, **Mary Jo Salter** is the author of five volumes of poetry: *Henry Purcell in Japan* (1985), *Unfinished Painting* (1989), *Sunday Skaters* (1994), *A Kiss in Space* (1999), and most recently, *An Open Book* (2003). A frequent resident at the McDowell Colony in New Hampshire, Salter, who was born in Grand Rapids, Michigan, in 1954, has received many awards, including a Guggenheim Fellowship, the Peter Lavan Award from the Academy of American Poets, and the Amy Lowell Poetry Scholarship. She is currently the Emily Dickinson Lecturer in the Humanities at Mount Holyoke College in South Hadley, Massachusetts.

Born into an impoverished family of Swedish immigrants in Galesburg, Illinois, and forced to take menial jobs to supplement the family income, **Carl Sandburg** (1878–1967) dropped out of school at thirteen. He served in Puerto Rico with the army in the Mexican War in 1898 and afterwards briefly attended Lombard College in Illinois, where a literature professor helped him self-publish his first three volumes of poetry. While working at numerous odd jobs, Sandburg became active in the Social Democratic Party and began developing the populist, folksy views that endeared him to the American people (though not always to other American poets) for decades. In 1908, he married Paula Steichen, the sister of the famous photographer, and, after moving to Chicago in 1912, began his literary career in earnest, writing for socialist papers and finding his poetic voice in a series of urban poems that *Poetry* magazine published in 1914 and which evolved into his "breakout" collection, *Chicago Poems* (1916). He devoted many years to his six-volume biography of Abraham Lincoln, which won a Pulitzer Prize in 1939. The author of numerous books of prose and poetry, he won a second Pulitzer in 1950 for his *Complete Poems*.

A prolific poet, novelist, and memoirist, the Belgium-born **Eleanore Marie (May) Sarton** (1912–1995) came to the U.S. with her parents at the age of four to escape the Wehrmacht invasion. She grew up in Cambridge, Massachusetts, and published her first poetry at the age of seventeen, when she also left home to join New York's Civic Repertory Theater. In 1933, she founded her own repertory theater in Hartford, but when that failed, she left acting and returned to writing. Her first collection, *Encounter in April*, appeared in 1937 and was followed by more than a dozen volumes of poetry, numerous novels, and a handful of autobiographies. She taught at Harvard and Wellesley before moving permanently to Maine in 1973. Her *Collected Poems* was published in 1993, shortly before she died of breast cancer.

One of the prominent British poets of the First World War, **Siegfried Sassoon** (1886–1967) left the luxurious, fox-hunting world of his wealthy Jewish family, along with the conventional confines of the Georgian verse he then composed, in order to join the Royal Welsh Fusiliers (in the same regiment as Robert Graves) at the outbreak of the war. A decorated captain, Sassoon soon turned against the war, publishing such powerfully realistic and satiric volumes of poetry as *The Old Huntsmen* (1917) and *Counter-Attack* (1918) that portrayed the horrors of the trenches and the futility of battle. In July 1917, in an open declaration to the War Department, he protested the war in what he called "an act of willful defiance of military authority." Sassoon's experiences form the core of Pat Barker's 1991 award-winning antiwar novel, *Regeneration*. At the age of seventy, Sassoon converted to Catholicism. He wrote several volumes of autobiography, most notably, *The Old Century and Seven More Years* (1938).

Like Keats's "To Autumn," Shelley's "Ode to the West Wind" is one of the great autumn poems of English literature, with its ecstatic mingling of wind, leaves, seeds, clouds, and sea, all becoming (including even the words of the poem) indistinguishable in a rush of imagery that attempts to imitate the impulsive force of the wind itself. A similar impulsiveness dictated Shelley's life. Born into a wealthy, aristocratic Sussex family, **Percy Bysshe Shelley** (1792–1822) was dismissed from Oxford because of his radical political and religious views. At eighteen he eloped with sixteen-year-old Harriet Westbrook, whom he abandoned, after she had a child, to then run off with sixteen-year-old Mary Godwin, the brilliant daughter of the philosopher William Godwin and Mary Wollstonecraft, one of the pioneers of modern feminism. When Harriet committed suicide, he married Mary (who wrote *Frankenstein* in 1816) and, to escape ensuing scandals, they moved as exiles to Italy, where in 1819, Shelley wrote many of his finest poems, including "Ode to the West Wind." In a note to the poem, he writes that it was "conceived and chiefly written in a wood that skirts the Arno, near Florence, and on a day when that tempestuous wind, whose temperature is at once mild and animating, was collecting the vapours which pour down the autumnal rains." Shortly before his thirtieth birthday, Shelley drowned in a sudden squall while sailing in the Gulf of Spezzia.

Penelope Shuttle was born in England in 1947 and currently lives in Cornwall. Her first volume of poetry, *The Orchard Upstairs*, appeared in 1980; other volumes include *Building a City for Jamie* (1990), *Taxing the Rain* (1992), and *Selected Poems* (1997). Besides several novels, she has also coauthored two books on women's lives, *The Wise Wound* (1978) and *Alchemy for Women* (1995). Her most recent collection of poetry is *A Leaf Out of His Book* (1999).

Maria Terrone, a lifelong New Yorker, is the author most recently of *The Bodies We Were Loaned* (2002). She has received many literary awards, including the 1998 Allen Tate Memorial Award, the 2000 Elinor Benedict Poetry Prize, and the 2001 Willow Review Award. Her work has been nominated for a Pushcart Award and has appeared in such journals as *Poetry*, *The Hudson Review*, *Atlanta Review*, and *Crab Orchard Review*. Terrone, a graduate of Fordham University, is the director of public relations for Hunter College in New York City.

One of twentieth-century America's most distinguished literary figures, **Robert Penn Warren** (1905–1989) is noted for his poetry, fiction, and criticism. Born in Guthrie, Kentucky, Warren graduated from Vanderbilt University in 1925, where he became associated with the Southern Agrarian movement. After earning an M.A. from the University of California at Berkeley and studying at Oxford as a Rhodes Scholar, Warren went on to teach and write, publishing a number of major-award-winning books; he received a Pulitzer Prize for both the novel *All the King's Men* (1946) and the collection of poetry *Now and Then* (1978), and the National Book Award in poetry for *Promises* (1957). A professor at Yale from 1950 to 1975, Warren published many books of poetry during the last two decades of his life. He is also well known for *Understanding Poetry* (1938), a textbook he wrote with Cleanth Brooks that is perhaps the most influential introduction to poetry for college students ever published; its methods of "close reading" are still critically relevant despite the academic dominance today of "remote reading" encouraged by postmodernism and deconstruction. Warren received a MacArthur Fellowship in 1981 and was named Poet Laureate in 1986.

Rosanna Warren, the daughter of Robert Penn Warren, was born in Fairfield, Connecticut, in 1953. Her volumes of poetry include *Stained Glass* (1993), *Each Leaf Shines Separate* (1984); and *Snow Day* (1981). Her translation (with Stephen Scully) of Euripides' *Suppliant Women* appeared in 1995. The recipient of many awards, including the Ingram

Merrill Foundation Award, a Lila Wallace Readers Digest Award, and fellowships from the Guggenheim Foundation and the American Council of Learned Societies, she is currently Emma MacLachlan Metcalf Professor of the Humanities at Boston University.

Verbally polished until they shine, **Richard Wilbur**'s poems have served as models of the poet's craft ever since *The Beautiful Changes and Other Poems* appeared in 1947. One would be hard-pressed to find a reputable textbook on the art of poetry that did not include a few examples of Wilbur's disciplined and exemplary work. Born in New York City in 1921, Wilbur was educated at Amherst College (where he studied with Robert Frost) and Harvard University. America's Poet Laureate in 1987, Wilbur won the Pulitzer Prize in 1989 for his *New and Collected Poems*. He has taught for many years at Wesleyan University and is also well known for his highly acclaimed translations of Moliere.

For several decades **Yvor Winters** (1900–1968) was one of America's most prominent critics and poets. Born in Chicago and raised in California, Winters earned his B.A. and M.A. from the University of Colorado and his doctorate from Stanford, where he taught for many years; his students included the poets Thom Gunn and Robert Pinsky. Winters was publishing poetry before he graduated college; *The Immobile Wind* appeared in 1921. His *Collected Poems* received the Bollingen Prize in 1962. Best known today for his criticism, which emphasized the importance of rationality and morality in literature, Winters waged a battle against romantic obscurantism in such books as *Primitivism and Decadence* (1937), *Maule's Curse* (1938), and *The Anatomy of Nonsense* (1943), which are all collected in *In Defense of Reason* (1947). He published *The Function of Criticism* in 1957.

William Wordsworth (1770–1850) was born in England's Lake District, a region that not only became his life long home but, largely because of him, a spiritual center of English poetry. Wordsworth's childhood was filled with loss; his mother died when he was eight, and his father, five years later. After his graduation from Cambridge and an ill-fated love affair with a young woman he met in France, with whom he had a daughter, the personal losses continued to accumulate: his favorite brother, a sea captain, drowned in 1805, and two of Wordsworth's young children died in 1812. In 1798, Wordsworth jointly published, with his friend Samuel Taylor Coleridge, *Lyrical Ballads*, a small volume of poems that became a landmark of English literature. Over the next ten years, Wordsworth wrote most of his greatest poetry, though his "great decade" is somewhat exaggerated, as over the years such splendid poems as the sonnet "September, 1815" would regularly appear. Wordsworth was named England's Poet Laureate in 1843.

The great Irish poet and playwright **William Butler Yeats** (1865–1939) was born in a suburb of Dublin. Throughout his childhood he got to know both London, where his father hoped to make a career as a painter, and the County Sligo countryside, where his mother's family made its home and where he developed the passion for Irish folklore that later resulted in his collection of essays *The Celtic Twilight* (1893) and his first volume of poetry, *The Wanderings of Oisin* (1889). While in Dublin, Yeats grew increasingly involved in theater, politics, and the occult, interests that would inspire and shape his work, as he continually reinvented his literary career, from the romantic pre-Raphaelite of the 1890s to the Nobel Prize–winning craftsman of the 1920s and then to the wild old man full of "lust and rage" of the 1930s. Yeats had met patron and friend Lady Augusta Gregory in 1896 and became a frequent visitor to her estate at Coole Park in County Galway, the setting of one of his most famous lyrics, "The Wild Swans at Coole."

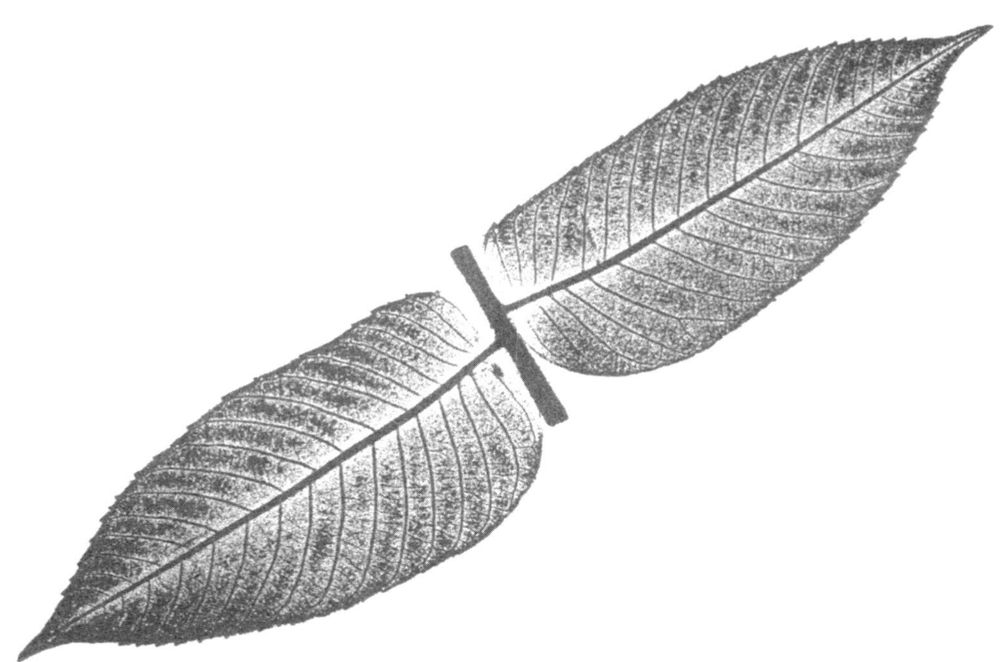

CREDITS

A. R. Ammons
"Equinox" from *Collected Poems: 1951–1971* by A. R. Ammons. Copyright © 1972 by A. R. Ammons. Used by permission of W. W. Norton & Company, Inc.

Star Black
"Auto-Autumn" from *Ghostwood* by Star Black. Copyright © 2003 by Star Black. Published by Melville House Press, Hoboken, N.J. Reprinted by permission of the author and Melville House Press.

Robert Bly
"Solitude Late at Night in the Woods" from *Silence in the Snowy Fields* by Robert Bly. Copyright © 1962 by Robert Bly. Reprinted by permission of Wesleyan University Press.

Louise Bogan
"Simple Autumnal" from *The Blue Estuaries* by Louise Bogan. Copyright © 1968 by Louise Bogan. Copyright renewed 1996 by Ruth Limmer. Reprinted by permission of Farrar, Straus and Giroux, LLC.

Marianne Boruch
"Leaves to Fall" is reprinted by permission of *The Iowa Review*. All rights reserved.

e. e. cummings
"[l (a]" from *Complete Poems: 1904–1962* by e. e. cummings. Copyright © 1994 by the Edward Estlin Cummings Literary Estate. Reprinted by permission of Liveright.

H. L. Davis
"Proud Riders" from *Selected Poems of H. L. Davis* by H. L. Davis. Copyright © 1978 by Elizabeth T. Hobson. Reprinted by permission of Ahsahta Press.

William Virgil Davis
"Leaves" first appeared in *The Gettysburg Review*, vol. 15, no. 1, and is reprinted here by permission of *The Gettysburg Review* and the author. All rights reserved.

Robert Frost
"My November Guest" from *The Poetry of Robert Frost: The Collected Poems, Complete and Unabridged*. Copyright © 1987 the Robert Frost Estate. Reprinted by permission of Henry Holt.

Jorie Graham
"Mind" from *Hybrids of Plants and Ghosts* by Jorie Graham. Copyright © 1980 by Jorie Graham. Reprinted by permission of Princeton University Press.

Pamela Steed Hill
"September Pitch" is reprinted by permission of the author. All rights reserved.

Patricia Hooper
"Equinox" is reprinted by permission from *The Hudson Review*, vol. LII, no. 2 (Summer 1999). Copyright © 1999 by Patricia Hooper.

Archibald MacLeish
"Immortal Autumn" from *Collected Poems, 1917–1982* by Archibald MacLeish. Copyright © 1985 by the Estate of Archibald MacLeish. Reprinted by permission of Houghton Mifflin Company. All rights reserved.

W. S. Merwin
"Under the Day" from *The Pupil: Poems* by W. S. Merwin. Copyright © 2001 by W. S. Merwin. Used by permission of Alfred A. Knopf, a division of Random House, Inc.

Edna St. Vincent Millay
"Autumn Daybreak" by Edna St. Vincent Millay. From *Collected Poems*, copyright © 1934, 1962 by Edna St. Vincent Millay and Norma Millay Ellis. All rights reserved. Reprinted by permission of Elizabeth Barnett, literary executor.

Alan Michael Parker
"The Geese" from *Days Like Prose* by Alan Michael Parker. Copyright © 1997 by Alan Michael Parker. Reprinted by permission of Alef Books.

Katha Pollitt
"November 5th, Riverside Drive" from *Antarctic Traveller* by Katha Pollitt. Copyright © 1981 by Katha Pollitt. Used by permission of Alfred A. Knopf, a division of Random House, Inc.

Mary Jo Salter
"On Removing Summer from the Public Gardens" from *Henry Purcell in Japan* by Mary Jo Salter. Copyright © 1984 by Mary Jo Salter. Used by permission of Alfred A. Knopf, a division of Random House, Inc.

Carl Sandburg
"Falltime" and "Autumn Movement" from *Cornhuskers* by Carl Sandburg. Copyright © 1918 by Holt, Rinehart and Winston and renewed 1946 by Carl Sandburg. Reprinted by permission of Harcourt, Inc.

May Sarton
"The First Autumn" from *Collected Poems: 1930–1993* by May Sarton. Copyright © 1993, 1988, 1984, 1980, 1974 by May Sarton. Used by permission of W. W. Norton & Company, Inc.

Penelope Shuttle
"September" is reprinted from *The Republic of Letters,* vol. 11. All rights reserved.

Maria Terrone
"Firewalking Through November" is reprinted by permission of the author. All rights reserved.

Robert Penn Warren
"Heart of Autumn" from *The Collected Poems of Robert Penn Warren.* Copyright © 1998 by the Literary Estate of Robert Penn Warren. Reprinted by permission of the William Morris Agency.

Rosanna Warren
"Season Due" from *Stained Glass* by Rosanna Warren. Copyright © 1993 by Rosanna Warren. Used by permission of W. W. Norton & Company, Inc.

Richard Wilbur
"In the Elegy Season" from *Ceremony and Other Poems* by Richard Wilbur. Copyright © 1950 and renewed 1978 by Richard Wilbur. Reprinted by permission of Harcourt, Inc.

Yvor Winters
"The Fall of Leaves" from *The Collected Poems of Yvor Winters*. Copyright © 1960 by Yvor Winters. Reprinted by permission of Swallow Press/Ohio University Press, Athens, Ohio.